Historic SCOTLAND

DAWN G ROBINSON-WALSH

AURORA
PUBLISHING

HISTORIC SCOTLAND

ISBN: 1 85926 053 5

Distributed by: Aurora Enterprises Ltd.
Unit 9, Bradley Fold Trading Estate,
Radcliffe Moor Road,
Bradley Fold,
BOLTON BL2 6RT
Tel: 0204 370753/2
Fax: 0204 370751

Edited by: Dawn G Robinson-Walsh & Sharon Shipperbottom.

Printed and bound by: Manchester Free Press,
Unit E3, Longford Trading Estate,
Thomas Street,
Stretford,
Manchester M32 0JT.

With thanks to John for cover photographs.

Introduction

Scotland's history is as fascinating and varied as its scenery and people travel to the country to discover both. Tourism is a major industry today in Scotland, with old traditions kept alive at least partly to maintain the influx of visitors, although Scottish people also have a great pride in their heritage and try to preserve it.

Many consider the magnificent scenery of the Highlands to be the most unspoilt and beautiful of areas. The magic and romantic history of the region captures the imagination despite the fact that the Highlands as we know them suffered heavily from an ailing economy and from the clearances. The Highlands and Islands are certainly spectacular with their mountains and deep lochs and are well worth a visit.

Towards the Borders, the rolling hills form a far gentler landscape though not without interest. The major cities are Edinburgh, Glasgow and Stirling, the old capital. Edinburgh is renowned for its annual festival of arts and culture, while Glasgow has changed enormously over the years and benefited from its title as 'City of Culture'.

In some ways, it is ironic that most people know Scotland through its traditions - kilts, clans, gatherings of pipe bands and sportsmen, ceilidhs and tartans - ironic because such traditional symbols and pastimes were almost destroyed some two hundred years ago. The Highlands once contained a number of clans - 'children' of chiefs who lived on their land and owed loyalty to the chief rather than to the king. After the accession of William III , a Protestant, to the throne of England in 1688, many clans supported the cause of the deposed Catholic, James II and rebelled, generally unsuccessfully. The Jacobites had rumbled on for a number of years but in 1746, at Culloden, the last battle occurred on British soil where the Jacobites were defeated. The clan system was deliberately dismantled after Culloden by the English to prevent further rebellions. Many leading clansmen were executed, and the chiefs were deprived of military and feudal power. Weapons were confiscated; even the tartan was banned, and playing the bagpipes became illegal. The Highlands were further altered by the clearances - the clearing of the glens and straths to provide land for sheep to enable the now powerless clan chiefs to make a living for themselves. Many crofters were displaced to the coast to try their hand at fishing at this time. In 1814, an event occurred which coloured the issue of the clearances perhaps forever. A man called Patrick Seller ordered people to leave his land within six months. When they did not do so, he moved in burning townships, destroying crops and violently evicting people. An old woman who suffered burns died and Seller was tried and cleared of murder. The clearances developed notoriety and are still an emotive subject today in certain areas.

The other major violent historic event for which Scotland is known is the massacre at Glencoe. A new régime started by the Prince of Orange in 1689 was unpopular in the Highlands - some chiefs had been slow to take the oaths of allegiance to the King and Queen. Macdonald of Glencoe was one such rebel and the government resolved to punish him as a traitor. The punishment, carried out by the Campbells, involved the slaughter of nearly forty people though most of the clans-folk escaped to the surrounding hills. These days forty people is not many, but Glencoe has an air to it even today, and it is easy to imagine the treachery and brutality of the time.*

Scotland seems to have produced a number of colourful historical characters, often viewed romantically. From Macbeth (Duncan's General), immortalised by Shakespeare, to the poets, Sir Walter Scott whose popular poem "The Lady of the Lake" (1810) was based on the beautiful Trossachs area, and Robert Burns, originally from Ayrshire, thought to be the premier of Scottish poets, the country has attracted literary interest. Boswell and Johnson, and the Wordsworths were admiring visitors, along with generations of the royal family.

The Isle of Skye is said to be where Prince Charles Edward (Bonnie Prince Charlie) said goodbye to Flora Macdonald. The story goes that Flora brought Prince Charles to her house, Monkstadt, in the village of Kilmuir, after he had landed nearby. She was a Jacobite heroine who left Scotland for Carolina in 1774. Certainly, one of the most interesting characters was Mary, Queen of the Scots, whose reputation may be more colourful than the reality. It has been said that Elizabeth I of England did Mary her worst favour when she sent the Protestant John Knox to Scotland. Presbyeterianism flourished in Scotland under his direction and the dangers of successful Catholic rebellion eventually deminished. Mary's life story was one of wrangling with the Protestants, and claims to the English throne, but she is most notable to many for her marriage schemes and choices of husband. Her unfortunate life ended in her execution.

It is obviously impossible to give anything more than the simplest pointers to some popular aspects of Scottish history here, but the images and captions will hopefully point the reader in various directions to pursue at leisure. Likewise, details of the scenery of what was once known as Caledonia would be sparse and unsatisfactory - the best way to discover the magnificence of Scotland, its penetrating coastline, its numerous lochs, its hills and mountains and other more man-made attractions, is to visit the country and to spend time investigating its many facets.

Dawn Robinson-Walsh

* *There is still said to be an inn in the area which refuses to serve a Campbell!*

Chapter 1

All Things Scottish...

Even those who have never visited Scotland know something of its traditions - many of which have spread, along with Scottish emigrants, south of the border and to other parts of the world. Its products, such as whisky, which is one of the country's greatest exports, and haggis, are also renowned.

Whisky is the chief Scottish spirit distilled mainly from malted barley. A number of tourists follow the so called "whisky trail" where distilleries offer tours and sell their products. Dufftown is said to be the capital of whisky distilling and is the home of Glenfiddich. The distinctive taste of pure whisky is said to derive from the peat fires over which the malt is traditionally dried. Most whisky consumed is, however blended. The Scottish way is not whisky diluted with water, soda or dry ginger, but neat, or as a hot toddy, a traditional mixture of Scotch, hot water and sugar. It is then easy to see why its name derives from the Gaelic 'uisage beatha' (water of life).

Space does not permit the display of photographs of all the traditional pastimes and emblems of the country, but the following few pages pick out a few aspects of Scottish skill and sights still to be seen.

THROWING THE HAMMER - BRAEMAR GATHERING

The Highland Games are traditional athletics meetings which have been held since the early 19th century. They are usually of a professional standard. They originated from the custom of the clan chiefs trying to improve the speed of their messengers. The clan system evolved from land divided into tribes based on patriarchal lines. There were around forty clans at the peak of the system, along with smaller groups. Given clan conflicts, a speedy messenger was an asset and races were held to reward the fastest. A prize was given to the clansman who was first up and down Creag Choinnich, the hill behind Braemar. The Braemar Gathering is the most prestigious event. The Games all include standard athletic events, but also the more unusual such as throwing the hammer, tossing the caber, and in the past, the spectacular hitch and kick jump, now no longer practised. Braemar itself is the highest village on Royal Deeside. Kenneth II came deer-hunting here, and the start of the 1715 rising was announced here. Queen Victoria was keen on the Highland Games which established the Braemar Gathering as a royal sporting event. Another famous visitor was R.L.Stevenson who visited in 1881 when writing "Treasure Island".

GHILLIE CALLUM, C.1924

A ghillie is a term for a Highland chief's attendant who would probably attend during outdoor sports such as hunting or fishing. Traditionally, the lad would be barefoot and may act as a messenger, but some of the ghillies (such as those pertaining to the Royal Family) would be well-dressed and personable.

A HIGHLAND PIPER,

C.1928

The bag-pipe was an important part of Caledonian life and became a military instrument, although its origins are ancient and traceable to Persia, Greece and Egypt. The instrument is notoriously difficult to play, consisting of an air-tight leather bag with openings containing tubes. Prior to the 13th century, it was probably mainly a folk instrument, but later became a court instrument and is now used ceremoniously at special events and occasions. It has a reputation for a harsh, monotonous sound, but can be quite haunting when played well. People tend to either love it or hate it.

Foursome Reel, c.1928

The reel is said to be one of the true national dances of Scotland, along with flings and strathspeys. Here, the foursome reel is illustrated, by male dancers in their traditional costumes including tartans and sporrans. The dance is both energetic and requires skill. It is a lively part of Scottish tradition.

HIGHLAND CATTLE,

C.1905

The native home of this cattle would be the upland region of western Scotland, although they are now seen in other places. The spreading horns and long shaggy coat plus sturdy frame make the animals an impressive sight but also hardy during the tough winters of the region. Such cattle would be adept at surviving on scanty pasture. Colours vary from black and brindle to yellow or red.

Chapter 2

Southern Scotland - Lothian, The Borders and Dumfriesshire

This area of Southern Scotland displays a variety of scenery, some of which is upland. It is however essentially still a lowland agricultural area, although some industries were set up following World War II. The area is known for its cattle and sheep-breeding, and the export of these to England.

The Border area is historically interesting in terms of relationships between England and Scotland prior to the union, which were more often than not, antagonistic. More romantically, the area is known for the border ballads of Sir Walter Scott and the notoriety of sheltering runaway English couples who clandestinely married under Scottish law at places like Gretna Green, and Coldstream.

MOTORBUS, JEDBURGH,
1929

Jedburgh was visited by Bonnie Prince Charlie in 1745, Robert Burns in 1787 and Sir Walter Scott in 1793. Also, Mary Queen of Scots spent time here in 1566. The abbey here never recovered from the so-called "Rough Wooing" of the 1540s, an attempt to force the Scots to allow the infant Queen Mary to be betrothed to Henry VIII's son, Edward, to unite both kingdoms under a Tudor monarch. Perhaps ironically, the countries were united in 1603 under Mary's son, James, when the succession fell on the Stuarts.

DUNBAR HIGH STREET,

C.1926

Dunbar is said to be one of the sunniest resorts in Scotland, with a fascinating coastline. A castle was built on the cliffs in 856 to protect against invasion. In 1630, there was a battle here between the English army under Cromwell and the Scots under Lord Newark. Cromwell's force of 11,000 men defeated the Scots after they were drawn from Doon Hill for a position on the plains where they were divided. Cromwell estimated that the Scots lost 3,000 men at the battle.

MARKET DAY ON THE SANDS, DUMFRIES, C.1904

Dumfries is an attractive and dignified border town, said to have a mild climate and notable for its apathy during the Jacobite rebellions of 1715 and 1745. Robert Burns lived in Dumfries from 1791-1796 and his remains were interred here. The town was embroiled in many early struggles which ended in the independence of Scotland.

GRETNA GREEN - THE FIRST HOUSE IN SCOTLAND, C.1931

This is where, of course, young thwarted lovers from England would flee to marry without parental consent. The ceremony involved a declaration in front of two witnesses, often performed in local inns or at the local smithy's. The law changed in 1856 to require three weeks' residence, and in 1940, marriage by declaration became illegal, so elopements to Gretna ceased. The tradition still fascinates visitors, however and most people stop here to take a photograph.

FLOORS CASTLE, KELSO, C.1911

Kelso was another victim of the 'Rough Wooing', and also the Reformation. Floors Castle is actually a little up-river from Kelso itself, and home to the Duke of Roxburgh. The original Georgian mansion was re-vamped (some say to its detriment) in Victorian times. It is said to be the largest inhabited house in Scotland, with a window for every day of the year many of which may be seen in this picture.

HIGH STREET, HAWICK, c.1913

Hawick is the largest of the border towns centred on this narrow but busy High Street, whose oldest building is the Tower Hotel, once house of the Douglas and Scott families but converted into a coaching inn in the 1770s. Notable guests have been William and Dorothy Wordsworth and Sir Walter Scott. Hawick has two main industries - wool, especially cashmere, shetland and lambswool knitwear, tweeds/ tartans and livestock from nearby villages and uplands. Hawick's most famous sportsman was international motorcycle racer, Jimmy Guthrie, killed in 1937 in a competition accident.

Bank Street, Galashiels, c.1930

Galashiels is a textile centre where local weavers created the basis of their industry by forming themselves into a trade corporation in 1777. Textiles reached their peak here in late-Victorian times, and tartans produced here were especially popular. The numbers of workers were dramatically reduced as trade fell off, and people were forced to diversify.

THE SQUARE, MELROSE,

C.1933

Melrose is the Kennaquhair of Sir Walter Scott's "The Abbot and the Monastery". It is an agricultural market town beautifully situated between the Eildon Hills and the Tweed, but it is its literary and historical aspects which mainly seem to attract visitors:- ruins of a Columban monastery, the market cross, Skirmish Hill and a beautiful church.

CHAPTER 3.

EDINBURGH AND GLASGOW

Edinburgh, the capital of Scotland stands south of the Firth of Forth. An imposing city, it has been called the "Athens of the North", home to various monuments and statues. Today it is particularly visited for its world-famous annual International Festival held in August, established in 1947. The festival was started as a way of bringing peaceful co-operation among nations as well as visitors and revenue. It is now a prestigious event, known for street entertainment, art and off-beat 'fringe' theatre and comedy.

The city is dominated by its castle, set on a 437 ft. rock. James VI of Scotland and I of England was born here in 1566. Much of the city developed along the grid iron plan of James Craig, including the famous Princes Street renowned for its shopping.

Glasgow in the valley of the Clyde, is surrounded by hills. It is an important commercial centre. The city has developed a reputation as a cultural city, quite an achievement given its previous reputation as an overcrowded place with slum housing in the Gorbals area. Shipbuilding was Glasgow's greatest industry with excellent steel vessels made on the banks of the Clyde - however, its industrial decline has meant that Glasgow has had to develop its commercial heart and tourism.

John Knox's House, Edinburgh,

c.1908

John Knox was the 16th century reformer who was largely at the heart of Scottish Presbyeterianism along Calvinist lines. Perhaps unfairly, he is known for his treatise "The Monstrous Regiment" which regaled against government by women, for which Elizabeth I never forgave him. It has been said that Elizabeth sealed the fate of her Scottish rival Mary, Queen of Scots, when Knox was sent to Scotland, the land of his birth, where he rallied against the Catholic monarchy. He should take credit, however, for his work in dulling the emnity between England and Scotland.

HIGHLANDERS ON PARADE, EDINBURGH CASTLE, c.1933

The castle and its grounds take up an area of five acres. The ascent to reach it is steep, via the "Lang Stairs", and it is usually cold and draughty at the top. The castle was inhabited by various Scottish sovereigns, including, Mary of Guise and Mary, Queen of Scots. The castle is magnificent and imposing, but it is easy to imagine the discomfort experienced by its past inhabitants.

THE FORTH RAILWAY BRIDGE, EDINBURGH, c. 1924

The bridge crosses the Firth of Forth near the island of Luchgarvie. It is a cantilever type bridge, which tends to be used for large structures with big spans which may be affected by wind. This bridge was opened on March 4th, 1890. The main spans are 1,700 feet each, the length is 5,330 feet and the height is said to be 354 feet, or at its extreme above high water 361 feet. The bridge was built by Sir John Fowler and Sir Benjamin Baker between 1882-89, and was the world's longest span until Quebec Bridge was built with the span length of 1,800 feet.

Princes Street and Royal Institution, Edinburgh, c.1916

Princes Street has always been considered elegant and is a major shopping street in the city, home to various High Street names. These days it is difficult to imagine people being able to walk in the road as in this photograph. The Royal Institution (later the Royal Scottish Academy) is a fine building with porticoes, Greek Doric columns, and a colonnade on each side.

GREAT WESTERN ROAD, GLASGOW, c.1913

Glasgow is the third largest city in Britain, and Scotland's biggest. It developed as a port for goods from the New World, firstly tobacco, but heavy industry and coal-mining also developed. Open to immigration for hundreds of years, it developed into a fascinating cosmopolitan city, but also achieved notoriety as a city of slums. During the second half of the 20th century, many of the slums have been knocked down, and the city has developed both culturally and architecturally.

MAIN STREET, COATBRIDGE,
C.1911

Coatbridge was the main centre for the Scottish iron and steel industry, and the centre of the Scottish industrial revolution.

SAUCIEHALL STREET, GLASGOW, C.1916

Shops with their imposing facades on this early picture of the busy Sauciehall Street before the days of the supremacy of the motor vehicle.

Seamen on the S.S. Morvada, Glasgow, c.1916

Shipbuilding was the greatest industry of Glasgow, which turned out every variety of ship from liners to barges, dredgers to battleships. Because of its qualities as a port, with railway access, and docks, Glasgow became a target for enemy air action during World War II which caused a great deal of damage. This photograph was taken during World War I.

CHAPTER 4

STRATHCLYDE

Strathclyde (meaning the valley of the Clyde) is effectively an administrative region, established after the 1974 local government re-organisation which includes the coastal area along the Clyde, and the Isles nearby, up to the Loch Lomond and the southern end of the Trossachs, and inland to include Glasgow (here included in a separate chapter).

It is an extremely varied region which encompasses sea-side resorts, industrial towns and rural areas, with many attractive stopping places for the tourist. It is readily accessible and one of the more highly populated regions of Scotland. On the west the climate is also milder than many other regions and adds to its popularity.

JARVIES HOTEL, ABERFOYLE

C.1918

Aberfoyle lies on the road leading north to the Trossachs, between Loch Ard and the Lake of Menteith. A village set in splendid scenery, it is an area associated with Sir Walter Scott's "Rob Roy".

War Memorial, Killin

c.1924

Another village with Scott associations - "The Fair Maid of Perth" describes Finlarig Castle, a ruin with an ancient beheading pit, which was a stronghold of The Campbells. Otherwise, it is a tourist centre, with a stone nearby marking the site of Fingal's grave. An area of forest and hills, the village is popular with winter sports fans.

Dalrymple Street, Girvan
c.1912

A holiday resort with a mild climate, long, sandy beach, sports facilities and entertainment, but also a fishing port with riverside harbour. A thriving fishing industry means it doesn't rely on tourism alone; other industries include woollen goods, potato crops and fishing boats. Local Girvan boat-hirers take parties out to Ailsa Craig, an island of isolated rock.

THE TAM O'SHANTER INN, AYR, C.1908

Tam O'Shanter was said to have ridden a horse back to front to Ayr when drunk, so it is a fitting name for an inn in the town. The coming of the railways made Ayr a place for the Scottish gentry to visit, being a seaside town with two and a half miles of esplanade and relatively convenient from Glasgow. Ayr is famous for its connection with Robert Burns, poet of local people who wrote a poem "The Brigs of Ayr" about the bridges which span the river. "Tam O'Shanter" is one of the best-known Scottish ballads. Burns became a Lowland Scots hero and the anniversary of his birth (25th January, 1759) is celebrated around the world with special suppers served on Burns' night.

INVERARAY CASTLE, c.1914

Capital of the once formidable Clan Campbell, Inveraray has long hosted traditional Highland Games in July. The Highland gatherings became so popular that they spread to the Lowlands as a test of strength and fighting ability. The castle was built by Robert Adam, in Scottish baronial style, and stands in finely wooded grounds.

Loch Lomond from Ardlui, c.1912

This is the largest of the Scottish lakes and thought by many to be the most beautiful. It is 24 miles long and 5 miles at its widest point. Its greatest depth is 623 feet. It is a popular tourist attraction, and there are many small resorts on its shores. The scenery, when viewed from a boat on the loch, is spectacular.

Glasgow Road, Paisley,

c.1917

Paisley was originally a village centred on its 12th century abbey and the town grew from this. Important for manufacturing, it became a centre for cloth:- linen, lawn, silk-gauze and calico printing. Paisley print is still popular, but the famous, imitation cashmere Paisley shawls are virtually extinct. The town contained a number of mills and warehouses with the new town occupying much of the old abbey grounds.

THE CROSS HAMILTON,

C.1919

Hamilton was a town whose growth was based on the discovery of coal. Iron foundries and various engineering works also flourished but by the 1940s, all of the pits had closed down, and the town became mainly a residential and shopping area.

VICTORIA ESPLANADE, LARGS, C.1923

Situated 30 miles north of Ayr on the Firth of Clyde, Alexander III defeated a Viking battle fleet here in 1263, where they gave up control of all the Hebrides other than Orkney and Shetland. A mound covers remains, thought to be Norwegian. As visible from the photograph, the town has a long, pebble beach and is a popular seaside resort, with ample opportunities for sailing. The esplanade is 2 miles long and quite broad, running northward around the bay.

Rothesay West, Isle of Bute, c.1920

Bute is the biggest island after Arran. Rothesay, on the Isle of Bute, was once a spa, and is now a popular resort and yachting centre. Bute is fifteen miles long and three miles wide, separated from Argyll by the Kyles of Bute, a beautiful winding strait. Rothesay was fortunate to have Loch Fad nearby which was used to power the first cotton-spinning mill erected in Scotland, providing local work for people.

THE HARBOUR, OBAN,

C.1911

A resort, popular with tourists, south of Fort William. Dr. Johnson & James Boswell stayed here in 1773 when it was little more than a village. It developed into a town with the arrival of the railways and the proximity of several attractions. It remains a port for Hebridean islands, such as Mull. This picture offers a clear view of the imposing "McCaig's Foilly", a building like a colosseum which was begun in the 1890s by a local banker, John McCaig, to relieve unemployment. It is made of granite and unfinished but is a well-known landmark.

CORRAN ESPLANADE, OBAN, C.1932

One of the attractions of Oban is the story of Fingal. At the north end of the bay, the ruin of Dunollie castle, stronghold of the Macdougalls, houses a huge rock called the Dog stone, from the legend that Fingal used to fasten his dog, Bran, to it.

Group of Currachs, Isle of Arran

c.1925

The currach, like the welsh coracle, is a form of skiff, once commonly used as small fishing boats in northern waters. The boats were well made, often using rushes and stronger than they looked, capable of enduring rough waters. The design probably originates from the Norse raiders who found a home in Arran.

Loch Fyne, Inveraray,

c.1918

Inveraray is an elegant town whose northern aspect faces Loch Fyne offering a wonderful view of the loch. Situated at the northern end of the loch, it is a gateway to nature trails, mountains and forests en route to Loch Lomond.

Tarbert from East Loch Fyne, c.1909

Tarbert is situated at the shore of Loch Fyne on a land locked bay. It was once the centre of the Loch Fyne herring industry, but is now a busy, attractive resort. There are remains of a 15th century castle above the village, built to repel Viking invaders.

RAILWAY STATION BOOKSTALL, OBAN, c.1922

Rarely are railway stations such well-tended places these days - note the various hanging baskets of flowers and greenery. One thing hasn't changed - the presence of the Scottish company, John Menzies, whose stores are still a presence at most railway stations.

PIER ROAD, DUNOON,

C.1905

Beautifully situated between the Cowal Hills and the sea, Dunoon became a popular west coast sea-side resort with villas and esplanade. Above the pier stand the remains of the old castle which was visited by Mary, Queen of Scots in 1563. A local landmark marks the site of the massacre of the local clan by the Campbells in 1646.

SANDCASTLE COMPETITION, MILLPORT, 1910

A splendid photograph of some very imaginative sand-castles with their various adornments, and proud parents standing by. The days of bikinis and swimsuits had not yet arrived - it is difficult to imagine boys in ties and people in full daily costume enjoying the beach today. Millport, a popular resort, is situated south of Largs on the Firth of the Clyde.

Alloway, Ayr,

c.1922

Alloway's main claim to fame is as the birthplace of the poet, Robert Burns. He was born in a thatched cottage here in the 18th century, which attracts a number of visitors each year. Various mementoes and personal belongings of the poet are on view in the adjacent museum. Alloway is about two miles south of Ayr. Unlike many major poets, Burns' young life was one of straitened circumstances and hard work, but his gift for writing and love of reading won through and he became a prolific writer.

LIVINGSTONE'S BIRTHPLACE, BLANTYRE, C.1908

Another great Scottish achiever, David Livingstone was born in a small single-roomed house here in 1813, and worked in the local mills from the age of ten. Against the odds and with great effort, he qualified as a doctor in 1840. He had decided on missionary work in China, but was instead sent to Africa where he achieved fame for his explorations along with H.M. Stanley. His travels covered a third of Africa and were a great addition to geographical knowledge of the continent. He unfortunately died from dysentery in 1873.

Ardrishaig Harbour with S.S. Columba at the Pier, c.1911

Situated on the shores of Loch Gilp which runs into Loch Fyne, Ardrishaig is not far from the popular tourist area around Lochgilphead.

CHAPTER 5

CENTRAL AND EASTERN REGION

The Eastern area of Scotland always somehow seems more austere than the western side. This may be partly because of climate which is generally harsher to the east, but also because of a change in building materials with granite being popular in cities like Aberdeen, and even Edinburgh having its fair share of imposing stone buildings, some blackened with age, dominating the city. Moving towards the centre of the country the scenery changes again becoming more picturesque and gentle, but still home to an often turbulent past.

VICAR STREET, FALKIRK, c.1932

Falkirk is known for two battles, in 1298 and 1746. The first was a bloody battle between the Scots and the invading English. The Scots were doing well until Edward I brought in his Welsh archers who wreaked havoc and badly weakened the disorganised opposing ranks. This is said to have been the first victory of the longbow in a major battle. The second involved the Jacobites who defeated the government troops under General Hawley, breaking the dragoons attacking uphill in atrocious weather, and routing the infantry so that Hawley fell back to Edinburgh with heavy losses.

BALMORAL CASTLE,
C.1911

Victoria and Albert rented Balmoral for a number of years because the climate was more clement than in Invernesshire. In 1852, Albert finally bought the estate. The 1853 building work started on the granite castle with its 100 feet turreted tower, and new gardens were created as part of a working estate. It remains the Royal Family's private Scottish home, but is open to the public during the Summer.

Fish Market, Aberdeen

c.1910

Aberdeen, or "The Granite City" is the third city in Scotland, built largely of grey granite. It is a coastal city, and has also been called "The Silver City by the Sea", and more recently "Oil City" due to the helicopters running all day shuttle services to production platforms in the North Sea. Fishing has been one of the major industries. The fish market pictured here was opened in 1889, half a mile in length and 52 feet wide.

WEST ESPLANADE, HELENSBURGH, C.1930

The seaside resort on the Firth of Clyde was named, in 1802, after Helen, the sister of the Earl of Sunderland. Its famous son is John Logie Baird, the television pioneer and inventor.

HIGH STREET, ARBROATH,

C.1920

Arbroath is a fishing town, known for its product the "Arbroath smokie" haddock. An interesting piece of coastline, with cliffs and caves, it was once used by smugglers. The sandy beaches make it an area popular with tourists. The High Street houses the ruins of an abbey, once one of the richest in Scotland.

BALLATER FROM CRAIG COILLACH, C.1914

An aerial view of "the township by the river" which is 670 feet above sea level on the left bank of the Dee. The fine bridge across the river is to the foreground of this picture. Ballater, a granite town, close to Balmoral, was founded in 1770 to provide accomodation for visitors to the mineral wells nearby. It is a fairly popular summer resort with local people.

HIGH STREET, PERTH,

C.1913

Perth is an inland port on the River Tay. In 1396, it was the scene of a formal battle between two clans, each side represented by 30 men who fought each other to the death. It was the capital of Scotland until c.1452 and therefore an important centre. The presbyeterian, John Knox, preached his famous sermon here in denunciation of idolatry and his followers destroyed local monasteries here. In 1715, the Old Pretender was proclaimed king at the Mercat (market) Cross. A place then with a turbulent and bloody history.

THE CITY SQUARE, DUNDEE,

C.1929

The large square includes the Caird Hall with its fine classic portico alongside civic and commercial buildings. The city lost many of its picturesque buildings and narrow, winding streets and courtyards with modernisation; it now remains more of a 20th century city having lost some of its historic interest.

DUNDEE HIGH STREET,
C.1911

The 15 feet high Mercat Cross bearing a unicorn with the date of 1586 once adorned the High Street but was later re-constructed in a churchyard. In this picture, a busy High Street before the days of the motor-car.

THE ABBEY, FORRES, c.1892

Forres is one of the oldest towns in Scotland, and by coincidence, this picture of it is one of the oldest in this book. It once had a castle which has associations with the ancient kings of Scotland, Duncan and Macbeth. It was a town of early witch burnings, commemorated by the Witches' Stone. The ruins of the abbey are pictured here as a relic of this sandstone town.

MAIN STREET, CALLANDER, C.1929

A small town which owed much of its prosperity to its position on the road from Edinburgh to Fort William and Oban. It is also close to the Trossachs so catches the tourist trade - a very picturesque, scenic part of the country. The Trossachs is an area of beautifully wooded glen, famed for its beautiful scenery since the vivid description of the area by Sir Walter Scott.

MAIN STREET, PITLOCHRY,

C.1917

A rather pretty street open to travellers and tourists judging by the hotels and inns. To the left is a temperance hotel which would still have been popular around this time. The Temperance (moderation) movement was a response to the social problems caused by excessive drinking of alcohol in the 18th century, followed rules of abstinence and attempted to prohibit the drink trade - the movement had mixed success in Scotland, home to whisky distilling and a Presbyeterian stronghold.

THE BEHEADING STONE, STIRLING, C.1910

All land traffic to the Highlands was, in the past, forced to pass Stirling - hence, its fortress built on a huge, unscaleable crag was hugely important. The castle as we know it was built by the Stuart Kings with a birds' eye view over seven battlefields including Bannockburn. For many years it was effectively the capital of Scotland. James II and V were born here, James VI spent his grim childhood here and Mary secretly married Darnley here.

DUNBLANE CATHEDRAL,

C.1908

Because of the cathedral built during the early 12th century, Dunblane is sometimes called a city. Built on the site of a Celtic church, it was established by St. Blane himself in 600AD. Buried here are Margaret Drummond, mistress of James IV and her two sisters. They were poisoned, as a result of political intrigue, at a meal in 1502, a successful attempt to ensure that Margaret would never marry the King.

BRUCE'S STATUE, STIRLING,

C.1921

The castle was built on a strategic route between the Lowlands and Highlands. It was won in 1314 by Robert the Bruce after Bannockburn. The castle is approached from the esplanade where stands this huge statue of Robert Bruce. From this point, splendid panoramic views are waiting to be seen. The turbulent history of the area and its castle is also worth exploring.

DUNKELD STREET, ABERFELDY, c.1907

Burns wrote a poem based on this place called 'The Birks of Aberfeldy' about the wooded area outside the town, birk meaning birch. It is home to the famous Black Watch regiment, originally used to watch the Jacobite activities.

Starting Tee, Golf Course, Carnoustie, c.1911

Carnoustie is a small seaside town known more for its golf than its five miles of sands. The town developed into a tourist attraction on this basis.

HIGH STREET, CRIEFF,

C.1905

Crieff is where Highlands and Lowlands meet. This has not been a peaceful process! In 1716, for example, the Jacobites left the town a smoking ruin. Bonnie Prince Charlie, some thirty years later, held a war council here during his retreat to Culloden, which is said to be one of the most moving places in Britain as it was here that the Prince was defeated and lost 1,200 men. These losses were followed by a brutal massacre of the wounded, including many great Highland clansmen, such as the Macdonalds, Camerons, Frasers, Macintoshes, Mackenzies and Stewarts. Highland drovers used to bring cattle to Crieff market, but the town developed into a health and holiday resort during Victorian times.

SUSPENSION BRIDGE, MONTROSE, c.1914

This bridge across the Esk links Montrose to the Island of Rossie. The harbour lies between the suspension bridge and the sea. The town is primarily a holiday and golfing one although there is some industry. The Jacobites did gain possession of the town in 1745 and enjoyed some successes there. Back in 1716, it was this harbour used by the Old Pretender for his embarkation to France.

Post Office, Kinross,

c.1922

This is an ancient town associated in many people's minds with the art of curling. Curling is a winter team sport something akin to bowls on ice. Like golf, it is especially associated with Scotland. The wearing of a plaid tam o'shanter or similar is not only confined to curling in Scotland, but also occurs in other curling centres in countries such as Canada.

Doune Castle,

c.1908

The ruins of the castle which is believed to have been built by Murdoch. The castle has some claim to literary fame as it features in Scott's "Waverley"; it was also held for Prince Charlie by Rob Roy. The town of Doune achieved fame for its sporrans and pistols but also more mundane manufactures such as cotton.

MILL STREET, ALLOA, c.1911

An industrial and coal-mining burgh, with a small dock harbour area. Mary, Queen of Scots spent part of her youth here in Alloa tower and later re-visited it with Lord Darnley. James VI also spent some of his childhood days here.

Grocery Store Interior, Stirling, c.1918

From the days when personal service was paramount and stores would be well staffed with smart assistants, often male as in this case. It seems that shopwork was not always predominantly female. Note the extremely tidy looking shelves, the order note pads and the starched collars and ties of the young men behind the counter - a far cry from the hurried self-service atmosphere of the modern supermarket.

Newhaven Fishwives, c.1913

Three generations of fishwives starting from a fairly young age. The voluminous skirts would be functional and warmth would be achieved with the many layers of clothing and woollen shawls. The men would have the often dangerous job of going out to sea for their catch; the women would have the safer but messy and unpleasant job of preparing the fish.

CHAPTER 6

HIGHLANDS, ISLANDS AND NORTHERN SCOTLAND

The Highlands, in contrast to other parts of Northern Scotland, offer spectacular scenery with the Great Glen providing a natural divide between the central and northern Highlands. It is an area of hills and valleys, with mountains including Ben Nevis which at 4406 feet is the highest in Britain.

An area with economic difficulties, due to the problems in developing industries and the impossibility of most kinds of farming, tourism has been carefully developed and promoted in the region which effectively covers about half of Scotland. Along with the hills and glens, the Highlands have other assets - whisky distilleries, salmon and trout fishing, the grouse moors and deer which encourage people to visit.

Blair Castle, Blair Atholl, c.1920

The castle overlooks the village of Blair Atholl and once guarded a strategic route into the Highlands. Parts of the castle go back to the 13th century (1269), but it was mainly rebuilt in the 18th and 19th centuries. Home to the clan Murray, it was the last castle in Britain to be beseiged - in 1746. The Young Pretender had stayed here in 1745. Blair Atholl itself is home to an annual September Highland gathering.

HIGH STREET, NAIRN,

C.1920

An interesting picture of this coastal town. The harbour here was constructed by Thomas Telford in 1820. The town is attractive, with a good dry, mild climate. Many summer visitors come here for the sea air and, of course, the golf. The industries mainly relate to fishing.

JOHN O'GROATS - THE LAST HOUSE,

C.1920

This rather bleak and dismal place was named after the 15th century ferryman Jan de Groot and is thought of as the most northern point on Britain's mainland. In truth, this is Dunnet Head, which is not terribly accessible. Good views are afforded here of Stroma and Orkney, but there is little else to attract the visitor for very long. The North Sea can become quite violent and views of this expanse of water on a windy day are well worth seeing. It is of course the finishing point for those doing the Land's End to John O'Groats walk. The story of Jan de Groot is worth relating. Three brothers, Malcolm, Gavin and Jan, Dutchmen, arrived under the protection of James IV. They prospered and eight families bearing the name celebrated their arrival annually with a feast. A dispute arose regarding who was first. This was settled by Jan who built a house with an octagonal room and table so that they were all "head of the table".

CASTLE URQUHART AND LOCH NESS, c.1911

This ruined castle on the shores of Loch Ness in the Highlands was once a stronghold of the Grants. It dates from Norman times and was frequently beseiged and rebuilt. It was finally blown up in 1692 to prevent a Jacobite occupation. Loch Ness acheived infamy for its monster of which there has been many a sighting. St. Columba apparently saw and admonished it as far back as the 6th century. Certainly, it assists the tourist trade as many people visit hoping to catch a sighting of the affectionately named "Nessie". The Loch is about twenty four miles long, a mile wide and extremely deep. Its setting certainly creates an atmosphere - there may well be a monster.

HIGH STREET, WICK

Wick is a small burgh situated at the head of Wick Bay at the North Sea, not far from the John O'Groats. Its harbour was built, like the one at Nairn, by Thomas Telford. A centre for traditional industries - fishing, particularly herring, but also knitwear. It is an important link between Orkney and Shetland and the rest of Scotland and England. It was once a Viking coastal stronghold.

Prince Charlie's Monument, Glenfinnan, c.1930

Dramatically situated amidst the mountains, the monument marks the site where Prince Charles Edward Stuart ordered his standard to be raised in 1745. The monument was not actually built until 1815. An unmissable place for those interested in the Rising and the clans.

Foyers Pier at Loch Ness, c.1916

Foyers is a small village on the hillside close to Loch Ness, noted for its water-falls, so dramatic that they were used in the 1890s for hydro-electric power. Sightings of the famous Loch Ness monster have been reported from here.

High Street from the West, Inverness, c.1914

Inverness is an interesting town known as the "capital of the Highlands". It is at the north end of the Great Glen and not far from Loch Ness. It is a very old town, said to have been a stronghold of the Picts and was said to have been visited by St. Columba with a view to converting King Brude. The castle here has seen plenty of action and centuries of fighting.

HERRING GUTTERS, MALLAIG,

C.1921

Mallaig is a small fishing port with a Norse name meaning "gull bay". As many of the Scottish coastal towns, herring fishing has been a major industry, and the fish have been plentiful in the North Sea. Most of the catch would probably not be eaten fresh but would be cured by smoking as kippers.

DUNVEGAN CASTLE, SKYE, C.1932

The Isle of Skye is popular with visitors; it is easily accessible, and has a combination of marvellous scenery and interesting history. It has the romantic tale of Flora MacDonald's farewell with Prince Charles Edward to its credit, and Dunvegan Castle, home to the Macleod chiefs, with its grim dungeon and fairy associations. The scenery centres on the Cuillins. The Black Cuillins are fearsome looking peaks formed from basalt and gabbro. They are jagged as opposed to the more rounded red granite of the Red Cuillins. These mountains are spectacular and have been known to have a lovely pink glow at sunset.

EILEAN DONAN CASTLE, c.1908

This is the archetypal fairy-tale castle in a romantic setting on the Kyle of Lochalsh. It is linked to the shore by a causeway. This picture was taken prior to the 1912 restorations. Its setting is dramatic, at this junction of Loch Duich and Loch Alsh with forests, mountains and tidal waters surrounding it. Originally, it was built in 1230 as part of Alexander II's defence of the western mainland against the Vikings; later, it became the property of the Mackenzies, one of whom was involved in the Jacobite rebellion. Warships bombarded the fortress into a ruin while it was held by a Spanish garrison supporting James II's son, the Old Pretender. This place surely has to be on the short-list as one of the more romantic areas.

CALEDONIAN CANAL AT FORT AUGUSTUS, c.1921

The Canal was constructed by Thomas Telford and opened in 1822 and was the connection between the east and west coasts of Scotland to save ships the 400 mile journey around the stormy seas north of Great Britain. This was quite a feat of engineering and building to create a canal some sixty miles long (the artificial portion being around twenty two miles), with twenty-eight locks. Like most canals, this one fell into dis-use because of its small size and the increased power of ships. Railways and improved road links further eroded the importance of the canal systems throughout Britain.

CHILDREN SELLING SHELLS ON IONA, c.1920

This famous island is off the south-west coast of Mull. It has many historic connections with Christianity, most notably St. Columba who founded a sixth century monastery here. Here, local children are selling sea-shell necklaces to visitors, a helpful additional source of revenue for the islanders.